President Sophia

My Road To The White House

DR. ANDREW SASSANI, M.D.

ISBN-13: 9781974403721
ISBN-10: 1974403726
Library of Congress Control Number: 2017912763
CreateSpace Independent Publishing Platform
North Charleston, South Carolina

**This Book Is Dedicated to
All the Girls in America.**

Special thanks to those who marched on the
streets to bring voting rights to women.

Special thanks to all the girls who've stood up,
and continue to stand up, for the
ideals of a better America.

Special thanks to those who always vote
and make our democracy stronger.

Special thanks to all who stand up
for justice and equality.

Very special thanks and early congratulations to the
future First Female President of the United States.
(What took you so long?)

My name is Sophia, and I am 10 years old. Today, I'm announcing my candidacy for the President of the United States.

But, I am not just announcing my *candidacy.* I'm letting you know that this little 10-year-old girl, *is* your future President of the United States.

You see, for me it all started in 2016.

I learned that in all of American history, every president has been male and that we've never had a female president. I thought to myself, "Are you kidding me? This is ridiculous, we have to change that."

I was excited to know that Hillary, a girl like me, was very close to becoming the first-ever female President of the United States. It didn't really matter to me if she was a Democrat or Republican or something else. I was just excited that a girl like me, was not only in the presidential election, but was very close to becoming Madam President for the first time.

I must be honest with you though. Later, I was happy that she lost the election. I know it doesn't make sense at first, but hear me out.

My mom, too, was surprised when she noticed I was smiling that Mrs. Clinton had lost. When she asked me why, I told her that I *did* want her to win at first. But, later, I had changed my mind.

I had thought to myself, "If Mrs. Clinton wins, she would be the *first* female President of the United States." That would've meant, that *I* could never be the *first* female President of the United States! So, now that she has lost, *I* still have a chance to become the *first* female President.

Of course, that is if no one else gets there first between now and when I'm all grown up. I told my sister Olivia, cousin Emma, as well as my friend Isabella about my future plans. They liked it so much, that they too, want to become the President of the United States!

My parents told us that any of us girls can most-definitely become the President of the United States. Whether *I* will be the first one, only time will tell.

My mom said that after Mr. John F. Kennedy became president in 1961, he said, *"Ask not what your country can do for you. Ask what you can do for your country!"* Then she asked me, "So, have you thought about what *you* will do for your country?" To be honest, I hadn't thought about those things. But they were good questions and made me think.

She said she will help me figure it out, but the final decision had to be from my own heart and mind. My mom started teaching me that being the President is being a public servant. That means, the president serves the public. So, it is not about what is good for me or my family and friends. As the President, I will have to work hard to serve all Americans.

She asked me to think long and hard before making a "To Do List" for when I'm the president. She said that will be my "Platform" during the election. "What do you mean 'Platform'"? I asked. She explained that it is a list of important ideas and goals that a presidential candidate says she believes in and wants to accomplish for America.

She advised me to be realistic when I make my list. For example, my list cannot include giving every American a magic wand of their own. I realized that being the president is a lot more serious than I thought. If I am thinking of becoming the future President of United States, I must start thinking about how I will serve my country and its people.

I went to my room and started making the list for my political platform. I began by thinking about all the good things that make people happy, like having a pet dog, good friends, cheese burgers and pizza, play-dates, sandy beaches, nice dresses, and nice toys. So, I wrote them on a piece of paper and proudly presented them to my mom. "Here is my political platform for the Presidency of the United States", I exclaimed, and handed over my list. It said:

As the President of the United States, I will work hard so that everyone will have:

1. *A pet dog*
2. *Nice dresses*
3. *Good friends and lots of Play-Dates*
4. *Cheese burgers and pizza*
5. *Nice toys*
6. *Fun computer games and Apps*

As my mom read the list, I could hear her mumbling "hmmm", "interesting", "hmmm". I asked "What, mom?" She said that was a good list, but I needed to work on it a bit more. She said, this is not a list to help all Americans.

For example, what about people who like cats or birds instead of a dog. What about Americans who can't afford having live pets because it costs money to feed them and to take care of them, or Americans who can't afford "nice" toys, or "nice" dresses? And what about people who don't want to wear dresses or don't like cheese burgers or pizza?

I realized my mom was right. My list was too much about myself and left many Americans out. Without realizing, I was being a little selfish thinking about myself and the things I liked and not considering what others care about.

I said "But, mom, I don't know what everyone in America likes or cares about? How am I supposed to make everyone happy with my platform?" She said, "First of all, you can't make everyone happy or give everyone what they want. That's just a fact of life. And yes, you must be honest and truly believe in your own platform, but there are ways to improve your list."

With that, she started asking me questions which helped me improve my platform. She asked me if it'll be ok for my platform to say something like, "As your president I will work hard so that everyone has a good-paying job to be able to afford having a pet of their choice"?

"Yes, yes! That sounds really good. I like that!" I exclaimed. So, she and I went through the rest of my list and she taught me new ways of thinking on how to help others.

My mom also taught me that I can't expect people to vote for me just because I have a great-sounding platform. My mom said that I must get involved in our community and actually help people. My actions must speak for themselves and prove that I care about people.

So, we've made plans to visit a soup-kitchen, an animal shelter, a hospital, and a thrift store to see if they'll allow a 10-year-old to help as a volunteer. I know that there are many children who need clothes or don't have toys. So, I've put aside lots of toys and clothes to donate during my visit to the thrift store.

My mom also said she will take me to some political gatherings and maybe I'll be able to volunteer at a political campaign to get some experience and see how things work. She says it is very exciting. I can't wait!

By the way, I held my first political meeting of my own where I negotiated an agreement. I held a group meeting with my sister Olivia, cousin Emma, and my friend Isabella to see if we can come to an agreement on who will run for which office, so we won't have to compete against each other, but instead support each other.

We had a very passionate discussion. At first, we all wanted to be the President of the United States. But by the end, we agreed that I will be the President, Olivia will be a Governor, Emma will be a Senator, and Isabella will be Congresswoman.

We also decided to study the history of women in American politics and learn from them. My mom helped me with this research. Our research made us realize that we definitely need more girls in politics. Although half of America is female (50%), in 2017 women make up only:

- 21% of U.S. Senators
- 20% of U.S. Representatives in congress
- 12% of Governors

As for female presidential candidates, our research showed that no woman had ever come as close to winning the presidency than Mrs. Hillary Clinton in 2016.

But it all started a long time ago with Victoria Woodhull in 1872 as America's first female presidential candidate. That's close to 50 years before women were even allowed to vote. Victoria was very brave. The lady in the red coat is Victoria Woodhull. Although Mrs. Hillary Clinton lost the presidency to her opponent because of something called the "Electoral College", she is the first and only woman in American history to receive the most votes in a presidential election.

Isn't that interesting? She got more votes than her opponent, but it was him who won the presidency. That's because of how "Electoral College" voting system works. My mom explained what that means, but honestly, it's still a bit confusing and I can't explain it myself. If you are interested to know more about that, ask your parent or a teacher.

Our research also brought us to some of the first women in American politics who became Governors, Senators, and Congresswomen. My mom introduced me to a book called *Little Girls Powerful Women: How Girls Break Ceilings* by Dr. Andrew Sassani M.D. This book tells the true-life stories of many women who became the "first" in America, including politicians. I would like to tell you about some of them.

Jeannette Rankin was elected as the first US Congresswoman in 1916. She, along with Susan B. Anthony, Elizabeth Cady Stanton, Ida B. Wells, and many other women, played an important role in the passage of what became the 19th Amendment to the US Constitution which gave full voting rights to women in 1920.

Nellie Tayloe Ross became the first female governor in the United States in 1925. As governor, she supported laws protecting children, women, and the poor. To this date, Nellie remains the only woman to have served as governor of Wyoming.

Hattie Caraway won the special election in January 1932 and became the first woman elected to the US Senate.

Patsy Mink became the first Asian American woman to be elected to the US Congress in 1965. While in Congress, she introduced the Early Childhood Education Act and wrote the Women's Educational Equity Act. These laws improved the rights of women and children.

The president of the United States named the law after her, calling it "the Patsy Mink Equal Opportunity in

Education Act". She was also awarded a Presidential Medal of Freedom.

Shirley Chisolm became the first African American woman to win an election to serve in the US Congress in 1968. Her speech "For the Equal Rights Amendment" is considered one of the top one hundred speeches of the twentieth century. In 1993, Shirley Chisolm's name was added to the National Women's  Hall of Fame, and some years later, she was awarded the Presidential Medal of Freedom.

 Ileana Ros-Lehtinen became the first Hispanic American congresswoman elected to the US House of Representatives in 1989. Before entering politics, Ileana was a teacher. She cared about students, especially those who didn't have enough money to pay for college.

Carol Mosely Braun became the first female African American US senator in 1992. After her work in the U.S. Senate, the president of the United States appointed her to represent America as an ambassador to New Zealand in 1999.

Although she had been a congresswoman since 1988, Nancy Pelosi became the first woman, the first Californian, and the first Italian American to hold the position of Speaker of the U.S. House of Represen- tatives in 2007. With that, she had become the highest-ranking elected female politi- cian in American history. Forbes maga-  zine listed her as one of the world's most powerful women. During her speech, she talked about the importance of being the first female to hold the position of Speaker of the House, *"This is a historic moment…for the women of this country. It is a moment for which we have waited more than 200 years… through the many years of struggle to achieve our rights… Never losing faith, we worked to redeem the promise of America, that all men and women are created equal. For our daughters and granddaughters, today, we have broken the marble ceiling. For our daughters and our granddaughters, the sky is the limit; anything is possible for them."*

As for Mrs. Clinton who came very close to winning the presidency, it was to me and millions of other girls like me, when she said in her speech the following day, *"I know we have still not [won the presi- dency], … but some day, someone will…and to all the*  *little girls who are watching this, never doubt that you are valuable and powerful and deserving of every chance and opportunity in the world to pursue and achieve your own dreams."*

Mrs. Clinton may have lost the presidency, but she has also inspired many girls like me. Before the 2016 presidential election, I didn't know what I wanted to do when I grow up. But, now I do.

Victoria Woodhull started the race, Mrs. Clinton brought it to the finish line, and I will cross it into the White House!

I still don't know if I'll be a Democrat, Republican, Independent, or belong to another party. I guess I'll find my way as I grow up. But one thing is for sure, our country needs more girls to run for public office, and I will be one of them. I have given up being a princess and going for Madam President.

In the meanwhile, here is my new and improved "Sophia for President" platform:

As your future President of the Unites States, I, Sophia, will work hard to teach people that we must be nice to each other and be good friends. We should love all people, and hate no one. That way, we can have lots of friends and play-dates. I will also work hard for all Americans to have a good job to pay for:

1. *A pet animal of their choice*
2. *Clothes and toys*
3. *Delicious food*
4. *Clean water and safe neighborhoods*

I will also work hard so that every student has a chance to a good education, including learning how to build and write codes for computer games and Apps.

My name is Sophia, I love America,
and I approve this message.

Remember, I didn't just announce my candidacy. One day, *I am*, going to be the President of the United States. One day, *I*, that *"some girl in America"*, will be Madam President of the United States.

Ordinarily, **"The End"** would go on this page,
…but the story is not finished.

This is just the beginning!

Message to the Future President of the United States

I hope you enjoyed the story of Sophia's road to the White House. You've probably figured that Sophia was a fictional character created for this book. But, she is real in some ways. The future President Sophia is that *"some girl in America"* today. That girl could be you. That girl may be your sister, your cousin, your friend, or your classmate.

One of you girls out there will make Sophia's road to the White House come true and become Madam President of the United States. Our country needs more girls like you to run for public office and be in the positions to make rules and policies. From the Mayor's office to the Governor's mansion, from the U.S. House of Representative to the Senate and the White House, America needs girls like you to run for political office.

Many other countries have already had female heads of government, but not the United States. In close to 100 years since the passage of the 19th Amendment giving full voting rights to women, no woman has been voted to the office of the President of the United States.

How would you feel if everyone in your family voted on whether to get a pet dog or a pet cat, except you're the only one who didn't get to vote? That's why voting is so important.

Voting is what makes a democracy strong, and America is a stronger democracy today than it was before 1920.

No matter which election and no matter who is running for what office, as soon as you are old enough to vote, you must exercise your democratic right and vote. Every vote counts. Every vote matters. Every election impacts the future of our lives and country.

America is waiting for a girl just like you, to grow up and become the President of the United States. You can start by making your first political platform on the next page.

As time goes on and you get older, you can improve the list as you think of new ways to serve America. You will already have my vote. I'll vote for you!

And remember, America stands for Equality, Liberty, and Justice for all.

My name is _____,
and I'm running for President of the United States. As President, I will work hard to:

1. _____

_____

2. _____

_____

3. _____

_____

4. _____

_____

5. _____

_____

My name is _____,
and I approve this message.

About the Author

Andrew Sassani MD is a married father of two little girls. He is a Harvard trained Board-Certified physician and an Associate Clinical Professor of Psychiatry at a U.S. Medical School. His primary full-time job is being a father and husband. When he is not busy with his family, he is a full-time Medical Director at a national healthcare company. To follow or contact the author via Facebook (@LittleGirlsPowerfulWomen), click http://bit.ly/2w7ZuVH

Look for other titles on Amazon at http://amzn.to/2hsIE17

- *Little Girls Powerful Women (Parts 1-4):* How Girls Break Ceilings
- *Little Girls Powerful CEOs:* From Role-Play to Real-Life
- *Little Girls & Nobel Prizes:* America's Girl Power
- *BOOK for Girls:* Smart Words for Smart Girls by Smart Women

Made in the USA
San Bernardino, CA
19 October 2017